THINKING

THROUGH

ANXIETY

THINKING THROUGH ANXIETY

A BRIEF CHRISTIAN LOOK

J. Ryan Davidson

Ichthus *Publications* · Apollo, Pennsylvania

Our goal is to provide high-quality, thought-provoking books that foster encouragement and spiritual growth. For more information regarding Ichthus Publications, other IP books, or bulk purchases, visit us online or write to support@ichthuspublications.com.

Cover image under license from Shutterstock.com
Printed in the United States of America
ISBN: 978-1-946971-13-5

www.ichthuspublications.com

With thanks to God for giving me my
lovely bride Christie who points me to Him
in the fears of this life . . .

Contents

Introduction

This is a difficult world to live in. Who among us doesn't know that terrible feeling that can well up in us when we face a fearful or stressful situation? But for the Christian, this feeling can also cause us to doubt our faith in God. What can be even more challenging is when we wrestle with regular anxiety, fear, and worry. The unsteady and out of control feeling that comes with anxiety can almost overwhelm us as we sink deeper and deeper into our thoughts and wonder if peace will ever come. It is indeed a weary road for the Christian. Do godly Christians get anxious, we wonder? Can we still have biblical assurance of salvation and godly lives if we find ourselves in the midst of anxious thoughts? It can indeed be a real challenge, plaguing even, because the very comfort we need in those moments we feel is out of our reach specifically because we wonder if we are allowed to have gospel comfort when we are anxious.

For the Christian living in a cursed and fallen world with broken minds and sinful hearts, anxiety and fear is often a part of the journey. And for some Christians, anxiety will be more prevalent than for others. Therefore, it should not surprise us that the Bible, both in the Old Testament and the New Testament, addresses fear and worry in multiple ways. Fear and anxiety can be so debilitating. It can reveal our unbelief as well as show off our faulty thinking, and it sometimes demonstrates our physiological struggles. What hope is there in particular for those who seem to regularly experience anxiety throughout their life? It is from these questions we must turn to the biblical truth proclaimed throughout Scripture that no matter how strong our anxieties, fears or sorrows are in this life, they are but temporary, for soon we will be with the Lord face to face.

Recognizing a Real Challenge

According to the National Institute of Mental Health, it is estimated that anxiety disorders are the most commonly reported or diagnosed mental ailment in the United States affecting 40 million adults age 18 and older, or 18% of the population.[1] What is telling about this is not whether this statistic accurately reflects a biblical anthropology (i.e., whether one considers anxiety as a clinical disorder or not), but rather the sheer volume of individuals that report what are commonly called *anxiety symptoms.* The fact that for nearly one in five individuals to report some level of steady anxiety (for the diagnostic criteria require symptoms above the societal norm) shows that fear and anxiety have become commonplace in the average Western experience of life. And yet, the causes of such a reality must not be viewed as stemming from the exact same root in every case. As we shall see, there are a variety of contributing factors to anxiety, and it is precisely because of these factors that a well-orbed, yet scripturally dependent approach to our individual experiences of anxiety must be undertaken.

It is here that we would do well to follow the approach of David Murray in his helpful work, *Christians Get Depressed Too*. Although largely discussing depression, the same approach is helpful when considering anxiety. He writes:

> "There are three simplistic extremes that we should avoid . . . first, that it is all physical; second, that it is all spiritual; third, that it is all mental."[2]

What then are the causes we should consider when we think about anxiety in the life of the Christian?

(1) *A Cursed and Fallen World*

First, we need to recognize what fear is. Is fear always sinful? Seventeenth Century Dutch theologian Wilhemus á Brakel helps us to think about this systematically when he argues that all fear is not necessarily sinful:

> "Fear issues forth from love—either for ourselves or for God. Self-love engenders fear when something occurs which could deprive us of something good or whereby some evil could befall us. We fear deprivation, or the evil itself, and whatever or whoever would deprive us of that which is good or whereby

evil could be inflicted upon us. God has created self-love in man and wills that we make use of it. The law requires that we love our neighbor as ourselves (Mat. 22:39). It is therefore not sinful to fear deprivation and evil. This fear was inherent in Adam's nature prior to the fall, even though there was no occasion for this fear to arise in him. The Lord Jesus also had such fear (cf. Mat. 26:37; Heb. 5:7). One may indeed be fearful of death and other discomforts, and thus also of wild animals and evil men. This fear becomes evil, however, if it begets the use of evil means—either to preserve or acquire that which is good, or to avoid evil."[3]

There are some kinds of fear that are not inherently evil or sinful. In a basic sense, fear is the recognition or reverencing of the inherent power, status, and/or abilities of something or someone. We teach our children to look both ways before crossing the street because of a healthy fear or respect for how fast moving cars can impact us if we are struck. We have a certain God-given drive to live and we have a healthy respect, or fear, of death that keeps us from undertaking certain risks. However, most of our fears come from living in a cursed and fallen world with minds that are sinful. It is these very minds that we use to take in our place in the world. So, we may have a healthy respect for death that causes us not to take certain risks, but because we live in a fallen world, we also have to take precautions that our previously un-fallen first parents did not. For instance, we have to think about locking our doors, metal detectors at the airport, neighborhood watch groups and other similar precautions precisely because our world is fallen. This reality then has a way, for each of us, of becoming tainted with sin when we undervalue God's goodness toward and sovereignty over us and therein magnify certain realities to the point of sinful anxiety.

18

There is a difference in looking both ways before I cross the street, and refusing to cross the street because I am forgetful that God has numbered my days (Acts 17:26, Heb. 9:27). The latter is forgetting that ultimately, all things will work together for the good of those who love Him and are called in accordance with His purpose and that nothing can break us away from His love (Rom. 8:28, 38–39). The former is simply a reality of existence in our world.

(2) *A Broken Mind*

Sometimes regular anxiety can be the result of how the human brain can be broken by the sinful fall of man. While I do not agree with all of the ideas in his work on Obsessive-Compulsive Disorder (OCD), Jeffrey Schwartz has demonstrated that some aspects of Anxiety (in this case, Obsessive thinking patterns) are biologically connected. He writes,

> ". . . OCD is associated with a biochemical problem that causes the underside of the front part of the brain to overheat. In short, the person is suffering from Brain Lock. The brain has become stuck in an inappropriate groove."[4]

Arguing that in certain ways our brains get "stuck" or locked, is not new, but is a helpful consideration. In addition, we must not dismiss that anxiety patterns can often occur in familial patterns, and this tendency can often result in some kind of sinful behavior, idolatry, pattern, etc., which is connected to the way our brains work. However, if we can acknowledge unhealthy thinking patterns alongside a robust biblical understanding of fear and worry and its potentially spiritual origins, we will go much further in our struggle with anxious thoughts.

I know for myself, others, and many individuals that I have counseled often times learning a new way of thinking has been helpful with certain types of anxiety.

Specifically, I am referring to the kinds of thought patterns that get stuck in the mind of a person that seem to relentlessly remain such as:

- "What if I do get sick?"
- "What if I don't get an A on the exam?"
- "What if my perfectly healthy family member dies tomorrow?"

Sometimes these thoughts come in the form of questions. At other times, they are statements like:

- "The thought of killing myself won't go away, even though I don't want to harm myself."

- "I can't stop the image of _____ from coming into my head."

- "Because I had a quick thought of _____ in my head, it must mean I am a _____."

Most individuals can work through these types of thoughts, recognizing the areas of potentially sinful unbelief in God, idolatrous thoughts and/or they can come to rational answers to assuage those thoughts. However, for some, even once those things are handled in the mind, nagging thoughts remain, and there is the continual felt urgency, or need, to "think" about them.

In addition to sin, brain biology can influence the "how" of our thinking. On the one hand, we need to be careful blaming the brain or our biology for the "content" of our thinking in every way, thus ridding ourselves of the responsibility to think in correct ways (Phil. 4:8). On the other hand, a person with an anxious mind will be required to consider not only spiritual analysis of his or her thought through the pages of Scripture, but also will need assistance in recognizing that at times, our

24

brains will gravitate toward unwanted thought patterns. A brief perusal of their pastoral works will show that the Puritans were masters at this balance (works such as John Owen's *The Grace and Duty of Being Spiritually Minded*, or Jeremiah Burroughs' *The Rare Jewel of Christian Contentment* among countless others).

(3) *A Sinful Heart*

The Scripture declares that the human heart is deceptive and wicked (Jer. 17:9). One of the results of this reality is that we often set our hearts on idolatrous things. Think about Israel for instance, setting her corporate heart on various idols, and simultaneously denying the very instructions and promises of God. We do the very same thing today as did the Old Testament people of God. One of the results of spiritual idolatry is that we set ourselves up for anxiety. Allow me to explain. When we place our hope in things in an ungodly way (either things that are good or inherently evil) and those very things do not come to pass, or do not work the way we want them to, we experience feelings of anxiety. For some, this can become a lifestyle pattern that causes a sort of low-grade anxiety to exist as a newly formed habit. Not only is idolatry sinful, a byproduct is that the idolater can begin to live in a state of anxiety, waiting for their newfound "god", or idol to live up to the expectations that only the Living God can fulfill. One of the important things to take note of regarding the human heart is that it is often carried away by various things (Eph. 4:14), and as such, it is subject to disappointment and fear throughout life. We must constantly recall that the only true rock is our God.

Another reality to a sinful heart that contributes to anxiety is that we are often cold to the very Fount Who is our peace. A cold and dull heart often keeps an individual from pressing in to the hope that is found in the gospel and the work of God.

When spiritual coldness, apathy, lethargy or laziness set in, we do not rest in God or His promises. Our hearts immediately go after other broken cisterns (Jer. 2:13), which can never satisfy.

Oh how our anxious hearts need the regular experiential presence of the Lord through the Scriptures in order to be calmed and corrected in our fears, false assurances, and idolatrous ways. Even those with no physiological proclivities toward anxiety must realize that they are born having, and battle all of their life with, a heart that is sinful. We are prone to wander from the God we desperately need Who is our comfort in all of our fears.

Embracing A Steady Hope

So given the cursed and fallen world, broken minds and sinful hearts, where do we turn then? While this little booklet is certainly not an exhaustive look at the issue of fear and anxiety, nor how to be loosed in every way from its grip, there are a few foundational things that we can consider when we face such worries. Most of these things are spiritual reminders for the believer, but there are in additions to these, a few practical items that we will consider such as our thinking, and our physical bodies. If we consider all of these things together, rightly discerning our own situation, context and proclivities, through the Holy Spirit, we can find some growth in our wrestling with fears, worries and anxiety.

The Gospel Message & Repentance

It may not occur to us to think about the gospel of Jesus Christ when we experience anxiety. While we surely should not think that every anxious person will lose all their fear and worry by simply thinking about the gospel, the opposite reality is an absolute necessity to avoid; namely, that we should forget to think on the gospel in our moments of anxiety.

By *gospel*, I mean the message of the saving work of God revealed in the

Scriptures. This is the message proclaiming that God is holy, and that we are sinful and that God sent His eternal Son, fully God who put on human flesh and lived the life we are required to live—a life fully obedient to the law of God. This is the message that Jesus died on the cross and that as He did, the Father punished Him in the place of every sinner who would ever trust in Him. This punishment was the righteous judgment of God for sins. The good news of the saving work of Jesus Christ is the rock solid foundation to our very lives and identities as believers, and as such can be a balm, particularly in the midst of momentary worries and fears.

Sometimes, we must preach the good news to ourselves, and at other times, the solid hope of gospel implications can be a grid through which we examine our current spiritual state before the Lord. We should boldly tell ourselves that our righteousness is in heaven; that our sin has been taken away and that there is no sin that will stand against us in the last day. We are united with Christ because of His life, death, and resurrection and because of the sealing work of the Holy Spirit, we are treated in the courtroom of heaven as Christ is treated—perfectly righteous and accepted in the sight of God. Sometimes however, the gospel is a foundation for questions to assist us with our anxiety. Questions like:

- "Given that God receives sinners, have I repented of all known sin?"
- "Given that I am united with Christ, what can separate me from the love of God in Christ Jesus (Rom. 8)?"
- "What does the finished work of Christ on my behalf mean for this fearful thought?"

While simply rehearsing the gospel in our minds will not make every feeling of anxiety go away, or every worry-filled thought disappear, we certainly can find hope and comfort in it experientially, even in our most anxious moments. We also can find seasons of feeling fearful when we hold on to sin without repenting of it to the Lord (Psa. 51). As gospel believers, we will regularly realize sin in our lives, and should repent of it, and not doing so can lead to feelings of anxiety. Our ultimate hope in any situation is recognizing that all the benefits of Christ's work, to include our justification, adoption, etc. are bound up in Him, and so even the anxious person can rest in being "in Christ." It is also important to constantly have this reminder before ourselves, as often we may be tempted to see ourselves as simply "the anxious person," or to take on the "identity" of anxiety. We must remember that as believers, we are "in Christ," and therefore, our anxiety is not the core of who we are. Rather, being in union with Christ is the core of our identity now.

The Sovereignty of God

In addition to the gospel, we must also remember the sovereign rule and reign of God over all things. Our first parents began a pattern that we all are born into which is a subtle or flagrant belief that we cannot fully trust God. Often times even in the Christian life, this unbelief issues forth from a forgetfulness of His sovereignty. In our fears and worries, the "voice" we listen to and believe is not the Word of the Lord which proclaims to us that God is sovereign, that He does what He pleases, and that His decree will come to pass and will work out for the good of His people (Rom. 8:28), but rather that of sinful unbelief. Sometimes for many, God's sovereignty seems scary. In addition, we live in a fallen world where we can be the recipients of the sins of others, which can contribute to our worries, particularly if we have experienced traumatic events. Perhaps great suffering has come to an individual, and he or she cannot seem to muster up the response of Job when he buried his own 10 children: "The Lord giveth, and the Lord taketh away, blessed be the name of the Lord!" (Job 1). But do not miss the fact that these words were not said in a nonchalant way, but through the agony, tears, and gut-wrenching cries of a father at the graveside of his children.

Perhaps you have found yourself thinking that if God would order such a painful event to happen, how can we trust Him? This is what the anxious mind gravitates toward—the unbelief in the truth that the plans of God are for God's glory and our good. Let us remember the entire journey of Job. His living Redeemer would ultimately work things out for Job in a way that was good and right and would grow

Job in His own understanding of God. The sovereignty of God is something then that we can take refuge in and not fear (Isa. 41:10). It is the perfect ordering of all things by God who never changes, so even on our worst days, we will not be consumed (Mal. 3:6).

The alternative of course is that we have a God Who does not know the future; cannot order all things; is impotent when circumstances come; and is not independent but dependent on unfolding circumstances in order to act. But, this is not the God of the Bible. The paradox for the Christian is that we cannot always understand His sovereignty, and yet we can fully rest and trust it because of the character and nature of God. William Cowper, the eighteenth-century hymn writer, was right when he penned,

> "Judge not the Lord by feeble sense,
>   But trust Him for His grace;
> Behind a frowning providence,
>   He hides a smiling face . . .
>
> Blind unbelief is sure to err,
>   And scan His work in vain;
> God is His own interpreter,
>   And He will make it plain."

And even if our fears come to pass, we can remember the biblical category of lament— of lamenting forward in faith (cf.

Lamentations, Psalms of Lament, etc.).

The sovereignty of God is the friend of the anxious Christian, not his or her enemy. It is the rock solid conviction that God is ordering all things rightly, fueled by the Holy Spirit's work in our lives. This is a bulwark for the Christian in our deepest fears (Psa. 23:4; Rom. 8:38–39). May we long for the day when the night of our worries and fears are completely vanquished (Rev. 21:25) and our everlasting abode is one of complete fearlessness.[5]

The Ordinary Means of Grace *&* Sabbath

Whether referring to the issue of anxiety or not, every Christian should consider the biblical discussion of the ordinary means of grace. However, when we consider our own anxieties as those who are "in Christ," understanding the ordinary means of grace is particularly helpful in that they are a part of the regular spiritual diet for the Christian. When we say "means of grace," what do we mean? Late nineteenth and early twentieth-century Dutch theologian, Herman Bavinck defines them helpfully:

". . . external, humanly perceptible actions and signs that Christ has given his church and with which he has linked the communication of his grace."[6]

I am particularly thinking of the "ordinary" means of grace of the preaching of the Word, sacraments,[7] and prayer. These are the ordinary means or mechanisms through which the Lord births and sustains faith throughout the Christian journey. It is through these regularly-occurring means that the Lord strengthens and increases the faith of His covenant people. And it is precisely when we are anxious that we need not forget the blessings promised to those who come in faith to these means. Prayer itself is mentioned in the Scriptures as a resource in our anxiety (Phil. 4:6–7), particularly as the Christian casts his or her cares onto the Lord wherein the mind is engaged in a flood of giving thanks to God.

Often, when we feel anxious, we either consciously, or unconsciously believe that God is holding out on us. We are extra prone to forget the normal means through which He feeds His people, and we wander off from the green pastures of His provided food seeking to find other means. To be clear, faithful attendance to sermons, sacraments, and to prayer will not necessarily cause all of our anxiety to dissipate, but it may indeed diminish our worry. At a minimum, we need to be reminded that these means are for all believers, anxious or otherwise, and that we need not forsake them even when we are worried.

A part of this discussion on the "ordinary" means of grace also necessitates a brief mention of another related topic, which is the topic of Sabbath. [8] The ordinary means of grace are largely centered around the one-day-in-seven rhythm that the Lord has given His people. This day is a day of perpetual observance, not discarded with the advent of the New Covenant. This is a delightful day (Isa. 58:13–14), which is a gift to humanity (Mark 2:27–28) that points to the eternal rest, which is to come (Heb. 4:9–10).[9] This rhythm not only gives us a pattern for our days and how we spend them, but it also, as a God-intended byproduct, grants us rest from many of the things over which we could become anxious. Rest, God-centeredness, and weekly reordering of priorities are exactly what every human needs, anxious or otherwise, but particularly when the cares of this life weigh so heavily upon us. Consider the Sabbath and the regular ordinary means of grace as a helpful tool in the struggle with anxiety. It is when we are anxious that we are often prone to forget or forsake these good gifts of God to the believer, but in reality it is these very God-given tools that, while not necessarily curing anxiety, are what we need all the more when we are anxious.

Our Thinking

Our thinking patterns, broken by sin and the fall, are often the lion's share of the culprit for our worries. We so often fail to consider our own thinking, or thinking patterns (Prov. 12:25). The writers of the Psalms were masters of self-counsel and often demonstrated the ability to shift their own thinking patterns (Psa. 77:10ff). We often need to simply shift the focus of our thoughts (even regarding God, self, or others) to more biblically sound ways of thinking. This is the need of every believer.

Sometimes however, some individuals tend to have repetitive or obsessive kinds of thinking patterns. It is specifically here that I have encouraged many people with whom I've spent a fair amount of time in counseling, to first prayerfully analyze certain anxious thoughts and thinking patterns biblically. But for some, once a thought continues to invade the mind, often relentlessly, rather than continuing the repeated mental work of arguing with it, or entertaining it as something that should have center stage in the brain, following prayer, I encourage them to put it on the "back burner." By this, I help them envision my kitchen stove, perhaps at Thanksgiving time. Each year, my wife and I have a house full of people, and it requires a full stove all morning! Some items are front-burner items; items that must be watched carefully, stirred, and even continually seasoned. Other items, however, while needing to be on the stove to stay warm, are not front-burner items. Rather, since they no longer deserve attention, they are placed on the back burner—without being engaged further.

You see, for some Christians, try as they may with confession of sin, analysis of thoughts through the lens of Scripture, prayer, etc., certain, not directly, sinful thoughts will continue to abound. Those individuals cannot seem to get those thoughts "off the stove." So, rather than keeping them on the front burner, and constantly engaging them when they come, we put them on the back burner. It would be great if they could get them off the stove completely since we have already recognized multiple times that they are not true, irrational, etc. However, the minds of some cannot let certain thoughts go either for psychological or physiological reasons; therefore, we place them on the back burner and place something else (often times a biblical theme, Scripture passage, or attribute of God) immediately in its place on the front burner.

In the secular world, this would be labeled as a form of "cognitive restructuring" or "thought distraction," but I think even as we operate from a biblical perspective, it is a helpful consideration alongside a robust and well-orbed system of biblical counsel. This type of practice can be necessary, precisely because some people have thinking patterns which are the result—at least in part—of the way that their brains have developed. Are they responsible for the content of thoughts? Absolutely! But must they keep engaging a specific thought pattern time and again when it won't go away and is potentially getting further ingrained in their thought life? No. In fact, I would argue that the more we think about a front-burner issue, the further ingrained it becomes. So, we should ask ourselves if we *must* think about a certain unwanted thought.

If there are no biblical principles, conviction of sin, nor life-threatening reasons why we must, then we must not assume that because it is in our minds that we have to fixate on it. Rather, we put those repetitive thoughts on the back burner, and replace them with prayer (1 Pet. 5:7), scriptural truth, a passage to meditate upon, or even enter into an intentional period of thinking about another blessing that Lord has sent our way (i.e., our family, friends, local church, His provision, etc.). It may be hard to let go even after this work because it is still in the mind, but we are now less and less focused on it.[10] In time, that particular repetitive thought may even go away.

Concerning our thinking, Jesus' instruction concerning anxiety within the Sermon on the Mount (Matt. 6:25–34) is very instructive. There, we are asked to consider the fatherly care of our heavenly Father who will not fail to care for His children. We are also instructed to consider the futility of anxiety in that it does not further us, or aid us in our journey. Instead, we are to look at creation and the providential care of God over all things and realize that this care should bolster our understanding about "how much more" our Father will care for us. Jesus adequately provides specific areas that we can tend to worry over (clothes, food, our bodies) and in each one, He instructs us to think in different ways, or on different things in order to have a better perspective, paving the way to greater glorifying of God and the ending of our anxiety.[11]

In addition to these things, in general, we must also regularly consider the content of our thought life (2 Cor. 10:5). The Scriptures encourage us to think in certain ways (Phil. 4:8), and therefore, we must not simply be reactive to combatting sinful thoughts that cross our minds, but we must also be proactive. Are we regularly filling our minds with the things of God and His Word (Psa. 56:3)? Are we regularly considering His attributes, His faithfulness (Psa. 77:11–12) and His gospel promise? This is a part of the regular mind renewal to which we are called (Rom. 12:1–2). Setting our minds on the things of this earth will often produce great fear, worry or anxiety within us as well. Puritan Jeremiah Burroughs hits the nail right on the head when he diagnoses such as pattern:

"So, in the things of the earth, an earthly-minded man or woman has his or her thoughts filled with distracting cares about the world. First, looking upon the things of the world as such great things, they think that if they are disappointed they will be undone. They look upon it as such a fearful, insufferable evil to be deprived of their estate and outward comforts in this world. Second, they don't look upon the means of provision for themselves and their families as having any certainty in it, which is a main thing to be considered. As for outward things in the world, they find by experience that there is uncertainty in them. And then for any promise that there is in Scripture that God will provide for them and their families, alas, that they dare not trust. That's a thing that of all means they think to be the weakest. 'Lord, have mercy upon us,' they say. If they have nothing else to trust but a word of Scripture, they think of themselves as being most miserable and wretched."[12]

We must rest our minds on the things of the Lord, and not upon our own ways and understanding (Prov. 3:5–6).

Another component to our thinking is our growth in and understanding of the truth in the Scriptures. For instance, many often lack of assurance of salvation because they have mistakenly confused assurance of faith with the essence of faith.[13] Or perhaps they have confused faith in Christ with faith in faith, thereby basing their assurance on their own degree of faith.[14] This is just one example among many. Right understanding of the Scriptures helps us here with certain unnecessary fears that may arise.

Another contributing factor in our thinking is the overvaluing of the opinions of others. Sometimes we give an exorbitant amount of weight in our minds to what others think of us, or to fearing what they will think. However, the Scripture is clear that our views of the fear of man must be rightly placed under our fear and reverence of God (Psa. 56:11, 118:6, 130:4; Heb. 13:6). The fear of God is a good and proper fear and can help to align our other faulty fears. Thus, while we may utilize thinking strategies at various times, our ultimate source of truth for thinking and hope in the midst of fear is in the very Word of God and the doctrines contained therein.

Biology

As was referenced earlier, we are body and soul, and given the fallen nature and the world in which we live, we experience various infirmities that, while Scripture and spiritual means can often address, must be considered as a part of our battle with fear and anxiety. For instance, if we are experiencing increased anxiety, a good place to start in terms of our physiological reality is the area of sleep, diet, and exercise. There are clear connections between the types of food we consume and our tendency towards anxiety. For instance, most Americans consume a lot of stimulants (sugar, caffeine) and these may affect our anxiety level, particularly if we are already prone to such a battle. Perhaps an alteration in diet could help reduce some of the physiological symptoms that sometimes make us feel anxious. Second, the lack of sleep clearly makes our thought life more challenging, and a regular, healthy sleeping rhythm can often times greatly affect our ability to think aright, and to have the energy we need throughout our days and to be more calm in certain ways. Thirdly, a systematic approach to regular exercise can help us not only with our physical health, but can be a natural stress reliever. Regular exercise allows our bodies to release stress. This stress relief, over time, can aid us in our ability to handle challenges that come our way. All of this reminds us that we are dust, and as finite creatures, we have needs and limitations to consider.

Our biological make up and the inclusion of it here is in no way meant to imply that we can jog and diet our way out of the sinful aspects of anxiety. It is also not meant to imply that the Word of God is not sufficient for our Christian life. Rather, it is simply the admission that we are soul *and* body, and as such, we need to consider biological components. This considering, in some cases, may necessitate the need to consult a physician, and even in some cases, a psychopharmacological treatment (i.e., medicine). We currently live in a culture that too quickly wants to medicate every ailment, and in many cases, medication can be prescribed without proper analysis of the spiritual and psychological aspects to situations, not to mention the relational components that may be involved in a person's anxiety. However, we also cannot assert, in seeking to avoid this error, that there is never an instance where properly prescribed medicine, or other non-sinful biological treatments (nutrition, non-invasive neuro-therapy, etc.) should be considered. What is necessary though is considering how we as Christians think about such treatments.

For far too long, believers have left mental health completely up to the professional outside the church, and while there is wisdom in the common grace the Lord allows physicians and counselors to have, many of these professionals are operating on a foundation very different from that of the biblical worldview. Just take a quick glance at the foundational theories of some of psychiatry and psychology and you will find many idolatrous, or faulty premises (i.e., atheism, evolutionary biology divorced from a Creator, secular humanism, postmodernism, etc.). What we need is not an end to science, but rather godly, biblically informed practitioners who use their skills and training through a theologically rich and invested holistic approach that is not totally divorced from the local church. What if the average psychiatrist considered sin, gospel, and heart idolatry before writing a prescription? What if the average psychologist did not assume a positive psychology was needed, but rather a call to biblical repentance and faith? There is not adequate room to discuss all of these nuances here, but only room to advocate that while biology should not be left out, it should also not be considered as uniquely primary. For many, the common biological aspects of diet, sleep, and exercise are considerations that can at least start to aid us in our battle with anxiety. So, if you are taking medication, I am not saying that you are in sin, or should feel guilty. Rather, I am advocating that biological treatments be offered in conjunction with biblical resources and not seen as singular treatments.

Conclusion

The Christian, including the Christian struggling with anxiety, is united to Christ (Rom. 6). Christ is our redemption and sanctification (1 Cor. 1:30) and the Lord will complete the work He has begun in us (Phil. 1:6). Therefore, in our continual wrestling with fear, worry, and anxiety, we need to constantly remember, that we are assured resurrection and ultimate freedom from every sin and infirmity on the last day. Our struggle must be framed with the reality of who we are in Christ. This One, who will not bruise a tender reed (Isa. 42:13) is the One to whom we are indivisibly united, even as we battle with anxiety. Therefore, we have all assurance when He tells us to humble ourselves by "casting all your cares upon Him" (1 Pet. 5:6–7) that our Lord is with us, and that He is in control of all things. And all this we do, as we look toward heaven. Puritan Timothy Rogers wrote:

> "Let us always wait and hope for that eternal felicity which will at length dawn upon all the people of God in the great morning of the resurrections. At their entrance into heaven there will be joy indeed.

There is no night there . . . This world, because of its lowness, is subject to inundations and miseries, and innumerable vicissitudes of pain and grief; but that high and glorious world is the place of triumph and victory. Then we shall see our sin, which made us weep, be totally defeated; then we shall see that devil who tempted us be trodden under our feet, and never able to tempt us any more . . . Oh, what a glorious morning that will be that has no cloud to obscure its light, and will never be followed with a sad or gloomy night!"[15]

Our feeling of anxiety may not always be completely taken away by it, but a deep reflection on heaven and the Day to come can inform our fears, and the accompanying tears. For that day soon to come will see our Christ splitting through the heavens to gather His people from the four winds, and there will be no more anxiety, for we will always and forever be with our God and all things will be new (Rev. 21:1–5). And indeed, we will be whole in body and soul and our anxieties will be no more. What we cannot do is allow our anxieties here, no matter how strong, to cause us to doubt the efficacy of our Savior's work, the call to persevere in the battle with sin, nor His promise to come for us . . . soon. Oh dear anxious Christian, rest . . . rest, even amid the fears, for our Christ is coming. And when He comes, no anxiety will ever come to mind again (2 Thess. 3:16).

---

[1] "Facts & Statistics." Anxiety and Depression Association of America. Accessed September 25, 2017. https://www.adaa.org/about-adaa/press-room/facts-statistics.

[2] David Murray. *Christians Get Depressed Too.* (Grand Rapids, MI: Reformation Heritage Books, 2010), 11.

[3] Wilhemus á Brakel. *The Christians Reasonable Service, vol. 3 The Law, Christian Graces, and the Lord's Prayer,* ed. Joel R. Beeke, trans. Bartel Elshout. (Grand Rapids, MI: Reformation Heritage Books, 2015), 291–92.

[4] Jeffrey Schwartz and Beverly Beyette. *Brain Lock: Free Yourself from Obsessive-Compulsive Behavior. A Four-Step Self-Treatment Method to Change Your Brain Chemistry.* (New York, NY: HarperCollins, 1996), 7.

[5] Ed Welch's work is a helpful aid in considering anxiety: Edward T. Welch. *Running Scared: Fear, Worry, and the God of Rest.* (New Growth Press, 2007).

[6] Herman Bavinck, *Reformed Dogmatics*, vol. 4 "*Holy Spirit, Church and New Creation*," ed. John Bolt, trans. John Vriend (Grand Rapids, MI: 2008), 448.

[7] Within the Scriptures, there are two Christ-instituted sacraments (many use the word "ordinances"): Baptism and the Lord's Supper.

[8] A helpful confessional definition: "As it is the law of nature, that in general a proportion of time, by God's appointment, be set apart for the worship of God, so by his Word, in a positive moral, and perpetual commandment, binding all men, in all ages, he hath particularly appointed one day in seven for a sabbath to be kept holy unto him, which from the beginning of the world to the resurrection of Christ was the last day of the week, and from the resurrection of Christ was changed into the first day of the week, which is called the Lord's day: and is to be continued to the end of the world as the Christian Sabbath, the observation of the last day of the week being abolished. The sabbath is then kept holy unto the Lord, when men, after a due preparing of their

hearts, and ordering their common affairs aforehand, do not only observe an holy rest all day, from their own works, words and thoughts, about their worldly employment and recreations, but are also taken up the whole time in the public and private exercises of his worship, and in the duties of necessity and mercy." (London Baptist Confession of Faith 1677/89, 22.7–8)

[9] I refer the reader to the brief and helpful book by Walt Chantry on this topic: *Call the Sabbath a Delight*.

[10] Another way is to envision our thoughts as a "board room meeting" where we choose to consider more than one opinion at the table vs. automatically assuming that one set of thoughts, typically negative sounding ones, are true. Another approach is to not assume the thing that we fear is automatically true, but give "equal time to the opposite" of what we fear. For instance, if I have a doctor's meeting tomorrow to get medical test results, as I wait, if I assume the doctor is going to tell me I have cancer, until I hear otherwise, I need to give equal time assuming that he will tell me that I do not. Other questions like, "What's the worst that could happen?" where a person tests whether they are over-magnifying their fears, or the use of thought distraction by thinking

on more positive things (Phil. 4:8) can be helpful, but again, it is important to stress the primacy of the need to filter our thoughts through the Scripture. So, while these may be helpful, cognitive techniques to organize our thoughts, over and above this, we must rely first on the truth of the Scriptures and then, secondarily, consider how we think about our thought patterns in light of the Word of God. So the priority is the truth of Scripture first, and then second, our own thinking techniques.

[11] David Murray's book, *The Happy Christian*, may be a helpful resource here: David Murray. *The Happy Christian: Ten Ways to Be a Joyful Believer in a Gloomy World*. (Thomas Nelson, 2015).

[12] Jeremiah Burroughs. *A Treatise of Earthly-Mindedness: Showing the Great Sin of Thinking as the World Thinks Rather Than Thinking God's Thoughts After Him*. ed. Don Kistler. (Grand Rapids, MI: Soli Deo Gloria Publications/Reformation Heritage Books, 2013), 11–12.

[13] "This infallible assurance doth not so belong to the essence of faith, but that a true believer may wait long, and conflict with many difficulties before he be partaker of it; yet being enabled by the Spirit to know the things

which are freely given him of God, he may, without extraordinary revelation, in the right use of means, attain thereunto: and therefore it is the duty of every one to give all diligence to make his calling and election sure, that thereby his heart may be enlarged in peace and joy in the Holy Spirit, in love and thankfulness to God, and in strength and cheerfulness in the duties of obedience, the proper fruits of this assurance; so far is it from inclining men to looseness." (London Baptist Confession of Faith 1677/89, 18.3)

[14] "61. Why sayest thou, that thou art righteous only by faith? Not that I am acceptable to God on account of the worthiness of my faith; but because only the satisfaction, righteousness and holiness of Christ is my righteousness before God, and I can receive the same and make it my own in no other way than by faith only." (Heidelberg Catechism, 1563, Q. 61)

[15] Timothy Rogers. *Trouble of Mind and the Disease of Melancholy*, ed. Don Kistler (PA: Soli Deo Gloria Publications, 2002), 394–95.

Also Available from J. Ryan Davidson

For more information, visit www.ichthuspublications.com.

Made in the USA
Columbia, SC
05 January 2018